Including Children with Visual Difficulties in the Early Years Foundation Stage

Written by
Julie Jennings

National Development Officer: Early Years
Royal National Institute of Blind People

Consultant
Clare Beswick

Illustrated by
Charlotte Stowell

Published 2009 by A&C Black Publishers Limited
36 Soho Square, London W1D 3QY
www.acblack.com

ISBN 978-14081-1449-0

Text © Julie Jennings
Illustrations © Charlotte Stowell

**To see our full range of titles
visit www.acblack.com**

Acknowledgements

Special thanks go to the Specialist Teachers of Children with a Visual Impairment, SENCAN,
Essex County Council who shared their ideas on accessing the six areas of learning of the
Early Years Foundation Stage, Linda Hubbard, Service for the Sensory Impaired,
Cheshire County Council for play plans, and Margaret Nutt,
Nursery Nurse and technical support for Bristol Sensory Support Service
for the example of the plasma screen.
This book has also drawn on material that has appeared in RNIB publications and on
the RNIB's website.

Contents

Introduction

The term 'Early Years' is used throughout this book to cover the age range included in the Early Years Foundation Stage (EYFS): from birth to the end of the academic year in which a child reaches the age of five.

This book supports the principles of the EYFS. The EYFS is an inclusive framework for England that promotes a play-based approach within a rich learning environment. *Principles into Practice Card 1.2* states that 'the diversity of individuals and communities should be valued and respected so that no child or family is discriminated against'. We are asked to consider how a family arriving at the setting would know that all children are welcomed and valued. One way of showing this is by understanding the needs and requirements of all the children and families you work with.

When thinking about inclusion, you may want to consider this definition:

Inclusion is a process of identifying, understanding and breaking down the barriers to participation and belonging. (Early Childhood Forum, 2003)

We can all work towards inclusion by reflecting on how we enable children and families to participate and belong in the setting.

This book complements the EYFS by giving the reader an insight into the individual learning needs of children with a visual impairment or difficulty. It does this by considering the role of vision in early development and the impact of a visual impairment on early learning.

Throughout this book, different terms are used to refer to children who are blind or partially sighted, such as children with a visual impairment or difficulty, or children with sight loss. All references should be taken to mean that the child has a visual condition that requires special arrangements to be made to enable them to access the physical environment or learning activities.

Who is this book for?

Because visual impairment is a low incidence disability, many practitioners may have little or no experience of working with a child with a significant sight difficulty. This book will be of interest to all who are supporting children through the EYFS, including childminders. It is for adults who are working with, or would like to prepare for working with, a young child with a visual impairment. You may be working with children alongside their families at home or in Early Years settings, such as nurseries, playgroups, reception classes or out of school clubs. The materials can be adapted to suit different settings. In addition, it will be of value to practitioners from health, education and social care services who support children and adults in these settings.

All children need adults who are able to observe and reflect on their individual style of learning. Children with a visual impairment, in particular, need adults who are curious and imaginative about how they learn when vision is not their main way of learning. This book helps you to develop an understanding of the implications of a visual impairment for learning in order to give you the confidence to provide effective support to individual children in your setting.

This book considers how we use vision for learning and what the possible barriers to learning, are when a young child has little or no sight. It explores the implications for you and the child, and suggests some approaches that may be helpful in supporting learning. It makes suggestions about some aspects of developing and learning with a visual impairment that will enable you to provide a positive and responsive learning environment for the children.

The importance of vision

Most estimates suggest that around 80 percent of the information we need for learning comes through our vision. Vision provides continuous uninterrupted information. It is the co-ordinating sense that links the experiences of using touch, hearing and other sensory inputs. The brain combines information received through vision with information coming through the other senses (touch, hearing, taste, smell and the awareness of our position in space) so that experiences are whole. About 40 percent of the brain is devoted to seeing, which shows the complexity of vision.

Children use their eyes to make sense of what they are experiencing and much of what they see leads to incidental learning. Vision organises sensory perceptions of the world and makes connections. It is the way that the world attracts and engages the mind of a child. It also allows children to anticipate what is going to happen next.

How the eye works

To be able to see, three things need to work properly – the eye, the optic nerve and the brain. Working together, these parts:

- control the amount of light entering the eye
- control the direction of vision
- focus light on the light-sensitive cells of the retina
- convert light to nerve impulses that can be understood by the brain
- carry the nerve impulses to the brain
- integrate the information received through the eyes with information received through the other senses
- process and interpret the information that is received
- use the information to control and determine actions.

This is a complex process but one that most children and adults do automatically without being aware of it.

Here is a brief description of the main parts of the eye and their functions:

Aqueous
A clear, watery-like substance between the cornea and lens.

Choroid
The middle layer of the eye, composed of blood vessels supplying nutrition to the innermost layers.

Ciliary muscles
Attached by ligaments to the lens to adjust the focus.

Conjunctiva
The protective membrane covering the eye.

Cornea
The transparent 'window' at the front of the eye.

Iris
The coloured part of the eye in front of the lens and behind the cornea, which expands and contracts to control the pupil.

Lens
A transparent structure situated behind the pupil which focuses images on the retina.

Macula
The central area of the retina which is used for central detailed vision and for seeing colour.

Optic nerve
A collection of around a million nerve fibres which send messages from the retina to the brain.

Pupil
The circular hole (which appears black) at the centre of the iris through which light passes; the size alters to regulate how much light enters the eye.

Retina
The inner lining of the eye which receives the images and transmits them to the brain via the optic nerve; it is made up of cells called rods and cones.

Sclera
The white of the eye; a strong coat to protect the eye.

Vitreous
A clear gel between the lens and retina.

Visual cortex
The area of the brain responsible for processing visual images.

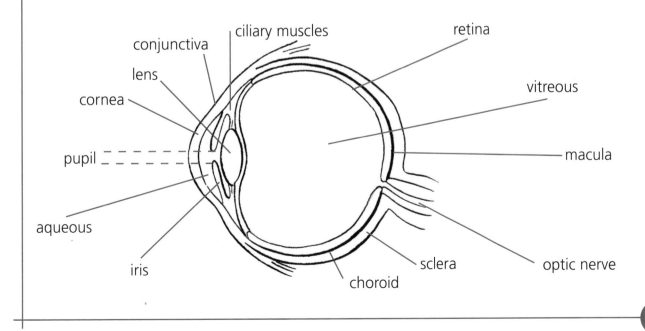

Early visual development

The eye is an extension of the brain. It is the most developed organ of the body at birth and develops quicker than any other after birth. At three weeks old, the parts of the body that are being used most are the baby's eyes. While a baby may not be able to control many body movements, the eyes are actively working and taking in information for them to use and learn from. Vision is still poor at this stage, so a baby needs objects that are of high contrast and which move. The human face is ideally suited to attract and hold a baby's attention and, even from birth, a baby is able to imitate facial expressions and actions.

Much of our vision develops in the first year, particularly in the first four to six months, with a major growth spurt between two and four months. Babies at this stage have been called 'robotic-looking machines', as their attention can be caught by more or less any visual stimulus. Vision is a learned process and, by their first birthday, babies typically have almost a full range of visual skills.

These include:

- seeing clearly both near to and at a distance
- both eyes working together (binocular vision) both near to and at a distance
- changing and maintaining focus both near and at a distance
- changing fixation easily from one place to another, up and down, and side to side
- remembering what they see (visual memory)
- recognising differences and likenesses
- recognising size and relationships in space
- recognising colour.

The development of visual skills, other sensory skills and learning in general passes through a number of key stages.

This is a sequence of visual development based on Kay Ferrell's work (see References page 59):

- First awareness, then attention, then understanding of an object
- First attention to light, then people (faces), then objects
- First fixation (looking at a light or object), then tracking (visually following a moving light or object)
- First peripheral (side) vision, then central (clear, detailed) vision
- First viewing part of an object, then viewing the whole object
- First interest in near objects, then interest in distant objects
- First interest in black and white, then colour (red and yellow)
- First preference for familiar objects, then preference for novel objects
- First interest in moving objects, then interest in still objects
- First interest in simple items, then interest in complex items and designs
- First interest in large items, then interest in small items.

Children's vision continues to develop in the first years of life and is considered to become fully mature around the age of seven. Vision develops best when it is used. A child who has some vision, however little, should be encouraged to use it as a part of all activities.

You can help by bearing in mind the kind of objects and activities that encourage looking. Ask the advice of the specialist teacher for visual impairment (see page 25) so that you can work together: it is always useful to have a second person with you to compare observations. Remember to give the child time to respond and repeat activities to check a response. If there seems to be no response, try again another day.

Visual awareness
Try to find a stimulus to which the child seems to respond. Movement is often helpful. Check any responses to sunlight, daylight, a camera flash, the room light switched on and off, torchlight, shiny objects, and black and white objects.

Visual attention
Check whether a child consciously directs – or avoids directing! – their gaze to gather information. This may be fleeting or sustained, but should be consistent. You can use the same stimulus as above, but you may want to link it to sound, such as a shiny bell or a Lullaby Lightshow, or touch, for instance, tickle games with sparkly gloves. Use language to help the child: 'here comes the light … now it's gone'. If you are using a light source such as a torch, always give it to the child to hold so that they understand that the light they may have seen is a real object.

Visual fixation
Encourage a child to locate and look at an object or face. You can try playing peek-a-boo, or hide and seek with a favourite toy.

Visual tracking

Try to give a child confidence in following moving objects with their eyes. You can play games with pen torches (with an Oogly on top), balloons or puppets, or try slowly rolling a sparkly ball along the floor for the child to catch. If the child loses eye contact with the moving object, stop until they make eye contact again.

Visual scanning

Encourage a child to find a particular object among others, or choose between objects. Start with objects that contrast in size, shape and colour, and work towards small differences. Make sure that the background the objects are on contrasts well, for instance, red or blue objects on a yellow background.

Visual discrimination

Support a child to see the distinctive features of a person, object or picture. You can help by naming some of the features, for instance by saying 'Paul is wearing his bright yellow jumper today. Shall we see if we can find him outside?'. Move from big to small objects, such as finding sultanas among dry beans, then encourage an interest in pictures.

Visual memory

This underpins learning: a child needs to be able to store and recall past experiences to match the images that they are looking at. You can help to develop recognition of a familiar person in a photograph, or encourage the use of objects for intentional purposes, such as using the bowl and spoon in the home corner to make a 'pretend' cake.

Visual spatial relations

Try to support a child in seeing objects in the environment (including themselves) in relation to each other, for instance, understanding direction, distance and orientation. This will develop their confidence in moving around their environment, inside and outdoors, using clear descriptive language, such as 'the ball is in front of you on the left by the tree'.

Visual motor co-ordination

Encourage a child to manipulate objects by using their hands and eyes together. Finger paints are good to try, as is playing with both hands in dough or foam, or finger feeding. Let the child control the activity, as some children do not like getting their hands messy. You can watch for any attempts at reaching for an object using vision, or how a child explores an object that they are holding. Do they hold it close to their eyes? Do they use hands and mouth to find out about it?

The main functions of vision

When our eyes and brain are working typically, then our visual system enables us to carry out nine main visual functions:

Focus

This is the ability to see objects clearly at different distances, both near to and far away, such as reading a book and watching TV.

Movement

Our eye muscles enable us to control eye movements, to move our eyes up and down and side to side in order to fix on objects and track them smoothly as they move.

Visual acuity

This relates to the ability to see fine detail, for example, to read small print, and is the visual function most commonly measured. The most acute area of vision is at the centre of the macula. When objects enter our peripheral or side vision, we automatically move our eyes to shift our gaze and bring the object into the area of our best central vision.

Visual field

This is the ability to see over a wide area. Working together, our eyes see in a broad field up and down and to the sides. Visual acuity decreases rapidly, moving from the centre to the edge of the visual field, but peripheral vision enables us to detect large objects and movement.

Stereoscopic vision

This is the ability to use two eyes together. It enables us to see objects in three dimensions and their relative positions in space, for example that our mug is in front of the computer. Binocular vision gives us the ability to judge distances and depth, which we need when walking up and down unfamiliar steps, for instance.

Colour vision

Typical colour perception gives us the ability to distinguish between blues, reds and greens, and mixed colours based on them. Our cone cells in the retina are responsible for colour vision.

Contrast sensitivity

Typical vision enables us to distinguish objects in poor light and where there is limited contrast or brightness between the object itself and the surrounding area.

Light sensitivity

The ability to adapt quickly and easily to changing light conditions is an important feature of typical vision. Rod cells in the edge of the retina operate in low lighting conditions, while cone cells in the centre are active in bright light. Consider how your eyes gradually adjust to the dark when you go into a cinema: at first you cannot see much, but gradually your eyes are able to see more and you know where to sit!

Visual perception

This is the brain's ability to interpret images and make visual sense of the world. It develops gradually and is related to other aspects of functioning, including the experiences we have had.

These functions usually work and develop automatically, but they can vary from day to day and will be affected by different eye conditions.

Visual impairment

Visual impairment refers to a range of sight problems, from mild to severe and total loss of sight. The number of children with impaired vision is very low. It is estimated that there are around 4100 children under the age of five with a visual impairment in England, around 4600 altogether in Great Britain (NFER/RNIB, 2008). Research indicates that the children with the most severe levels of visual impairment are more likely to have:

- been born pre-term or with a low birth weight
- a condition that is not treatable
- had their condition from very early in life, usually identified in the first year
- additional difficulties (Rahi and Cable, 2003).

However, children with a visual impairment are a diverse group. Each child needs to be considered as an individual, as what works for one child may not work for another.

Blindness or severe sight impairment

Blindness or severe sight impairment means a high degree of vision loss. Total blindness is rare. Most blind children can see something, but not very much. They may have a small amount of useful vision and be able to see light and dark, or they may be able to see movement. A child who is blind usually requires strategies for learning that do not rely on vision, for example, tactile means such as braille, or audio methods.

Braille is a tactile form of reading made up of raised dots. Children learn to write braille using a *Perkins Brailler*, a braille-writing machine with six keys that make the raised dots on special paper. Reading braille requires the ability to discriminate by touch the patterns that are made by the sets of raised dots, which represent letters or words.

The Braille alphabet

Grade 1, or uncontracted Braille, has 26 different patterns that represent the letters of the alphabet. Grade 2, or contracted Braille, is the complete Braille code, which contains the alphabet as well as 189 contractions and short-form words so that the Braille takes up less space.

In the same way that we read print to children who are far too young to understand letters and words for themselves, a blind child can feel Braille dots and begin to understand that words and Braille dots tell you what to say. You can help by having Braille around the setting. Sighted children will get used to seeing it around and may look for Braille in the wider environment, such as in lifts or on supermarket packaging, and you can direct a blind child's attention to it – by gently guiding their hand – so that they learn 'incidentally' that braille dots mean something.

From ClearVision Library (see next page), you can borrow books with both print and Braille in them, that children can share together. You can also add Braille labels to any print labels, making sure that they can be reached by the child to touch. You could also have a *Perkins Brailler* in the literacy corner for all the children to use. Your advisory teacher for visual impairment (see page 25) will be able to advise you on this.

Moon is another form of reading by touch which looks more like print letters, using curves and straight lines. It is easier for some children to read as it can be enlarged, but there are not as many books available and there is no easy Moon-writing machine for children.

The Moon alphabet

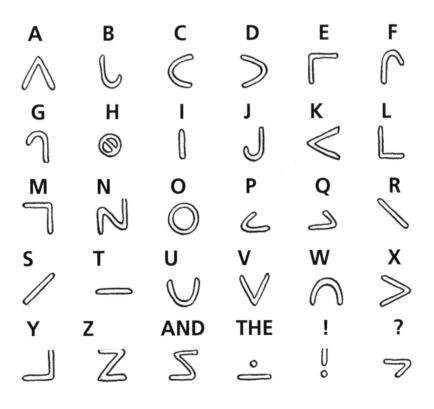

Resources for touch reading

- Bag Books sell tactile/multi-sensory story packs designed for children and young people with severe and multiple disabilities, and for pre-school children with visual impairments.
  www.bagbooks.co.uk

- Booktouch is part of Bookstart which aims to get babies and toddlers who are blind or partially sighted 'bookstarted'. A Booktouch pack is available free to parents or carers of children who are blind or partially sighted up to (and including) the age of four. These packs contain specially chosen touch and feel books.
  www.bookstart.co.uk

- ClearVision Library is a UK postal lending library of mainstream children's books with added braille. The books all have braille (or Moon), print and pictures, making them suitable for visually impaired and sighted children, as well as adults, to share. Titles are suitable for pre-schoolers and children learning to read.
  www.clearvisionproject.org

- Living Paintings supply a free library of living picture books and packs for children, and introductory packs of touch and sound books in three separate age groups.
  www.livingpaintings.org

- RNIB National Library Service has Braille and Moon books, as well as tactile books to borrow or to buy for children learning to read.
  www.rnib.org.uk/reading

Partial sight or sight impairment

Partial sight or sight impairment is a less severe loss of vision that cannot be corrected by wearing spectacles. Children who are described as partially sighted may have sight difficulties related to reduced fields of vision, or difficulties with seeing near to or at a distance. They may use enlarged or modified print and supplement this with learning by touch and using audio resources.

The size and font of letters makes a real difference. You can help by making sure that the children have print that they can read.

Examples of fonts and font sizes:

This is Arial Normal 6 point

This is Arial Normal 8 point

This is Arial Normal 10 point

This is Arial Normal 12 point

This is Arial Normal 14 point

This is Arial Bold 14 point

This is Arial Normal 16 point

This is Arial Normal 18 point

This is Arial Normal 20 point

This is Arial Bold 20 point

This is Arial Normal 22 point

This is Arial Normal 25 point

This is Arial Normal 14 point

This is Times New Roman Normal 14 point

This is Comic Sans Normal 14 point

This is Book Antiqua 14 point

This is Times New Roman Normal 20 point

This is Times New Roman Normal 20 point

This is Book Antiqua 20 point

This is Book Antiqua 22 point

Some of these fonts or sizes may be unreadable to many partially sighted people. Which one do you find most comfortable?

You can help by having large print books available in the setting. Here are some sources of large print books:

- Your local public library should have some large print titles for loan to children and young people.

- National Blind Children's Society sells a large selection of customised large print books to families and schools.
  www.nbcs.org.uk

- RNIB National Library Service provides giant print titles (24 point type) for loan to children and young people.
  www.rnib.org.uk/reading

You can also have audio stories available. Here are some sources of cassette tapes or CDs:

- Your local public library should have a range of spoken word cassettes, CDs and MP3s.

- Calibre Audio Library has a wide choice of full-length books for children and young people on cassette and in digital format available to borrow.
  www.calibre.org.uk

- RNIB National Library Service operates a postal library service offering recorded children's leisure-reading titles.
  www.rnib.org.uk/reading

Presentation of materials

You may also like to think about how to present written materials. It may not be an issue for younger children where print is normally larger, but it will certainly help some of the parents – and maybe staff! – who you work with. If you consider some of the guidelines below, it will help you to choose books that are more appropriate for a wider range of children.

This guidance is based on RNIB's introduction to its clear print guidelines. You can find out more on **www.rnib.org.uk/seeitright**.

Type size

The size of the type (known as point size) is a large factor in making print legible. RNIB recommends a minimum type size between 12 and 14 point.

Contrast

The better the contrast between the background and the text, the more legible the text will be. Black text on a white background provides the best contrast.

Typeface

Avoid highly stylised typefaces, such as those with ornamental, decorative or handwriting styles.

Type styles

Blocks of capital letters, underlined or italicised text are all harder to read. A word or two in capitals is fine but avoid the use of capitals for continuous text. Underlining text or setting it in italics should also be avoided.

Leading

The space between one line of type and the next (known as leading) is important. As a general rule, the space should be 1.5 to 2 times the space between words on a line.

Type weight

People with sight problems often prefer bold or semi-bold weights to normal ones. Avoid light type weights.

Numbers

If you print documents with numbers in them, choose a typeface in which the numbers are clear. Readers with sight problems can easily misread 3, 5, 8 and 0.

Word spacing and alignment

Keep to the same amount of space between each word. Do not condense or stretch lines of type. RNIB recommends aligning text to the left margin as it is easy to find the start of the next line and keeps the spaces even between words.

Reversing type

If using white type, make sure the background colour is dark enough to provide sufficient contrast.

Setting text

Avoid fitting text around images if this means that lines of text start in a different place, as they are difficult to find. Avoid setting text over images as this will affect the contrast.

Printing

Avoid glossy paper because glare makes it difficult to read. Choose thicker paper where possible. As a general rule, if the text is showing through from the reverse side, then the paper is too thin. (If you do find this happens, you can hide the image from the other side of the page by inserting a sheet of black paper behind the page being read.)

Checklist

Whenever you are preparing or choosing print materials, you can use this checklist:

- Simple and clear typeface is used
- Type size is 12 point or ideally 14 point
- Text is left aligned
- Layout is consistent and logical
- Words are not split between lines
- No large blocks of capital letters are used
- No italics are used
- No words are underlined

- No text is laid over the top of an image

- Paper is not glossy or laminated

- Paper is thick enough to minimise the amount of 'show through' from the other side

- Leading (the space between lines) is not cramped

- Good contrast is produced between the text and the background

- Line space is set between paragraphs

- All text is set horizontally

- No information is conveyed solely through the use of images, diagrams or colour.

Some common eye conditions in childhood

Difficulties experienced by children who have a visual impairment are not always obvious to the observer. There is a wide variety of visual conditions that give rise to a vast range of effects with many different implications for each child. Different eye conditions can create different ways of seeing: some affect seeing at a distance, others affect seeing near to; some will affect what a child can see clearly, others what they can see in their wider field of vision; some may mean that children do not see in colour, others may cause problems with glare. Many children with sight problems also have other needs or health issues that impact on their learning. It is important to remember that each child is an individual and even children with the same eye condition may appear to see very differently.

Some eye conditions are listed here:

Albinism
This is associated with a lack of pigment (colour) in the skin, hair and eyes. Lack of pigment may mean that tinted spectacles are needed to maintain best comfortable vision in bright light where glare is a problem. Albinism is commonly associated with nystagmus and problems with binocular vision. Children with albinism will have very short sight that cannot be corrected by wearing spectacles. Find out more at **www.albinism.org.uk**.

Amblyopia
Sometimes called a 'lazy' eye, this refers to an eye (or eyes) that has a decrease in vision that cannot be corrected with spectacles. It is usually caused as a result of an eye turn (strabismus/squint) so it is most likely that only one eye will be affected. It is very important that, if a young child has a squint, it is treated as quickly as possible when there is still the opportunity to improve the development of vision. Amblyopia without a squint is harder to detect so early eye examinations are recommended.

Anophthalmia
This is when a baby is born without one or both eyes. Find out more at **www.macs.org.uk**.

Astigmatism
This is an irregular-shaped cornea. Vision is distorted because the light rays do not meet at a single focal point. Very few eyes are perfect spheres so astigmatism is quite common. Depending on the severity of the astigmatism, the focus of vision can be corrected with spectacles.

Cataract
This is a clouding of the lens resulting in images becoming unclear. Cataracts can be present at birth or develop after birth. Most cataracts are surgically removed as soon as they are detected as ophthalmologists are keen to act quickly so as not to delay or prevent the development of vision in a baby.

Cerebral visual impairment
This usually results from damage to parts of the visual cortex in the brain and may involve specific processing and perception problems. It is very common in children with complex additional needs.

Colour confusion

This is not being able to distinguish certain colours from each other, sometimes called 'colour blindness'. Around 8 percent of males have colour confusion, typically with red and green.

Conjunctivitis

This is an inflammation of the conjunctiva.

Glaucoma

This is damage to the optic nerve, generally associated with a build up of pressure inside the eye.

Hypermetropia (long sightedness)

Things are seen more clearly in the distance than near to. This is typically corrected by spectacles or contact lenses.

Keratitis

This is an infection or inflammation of the cornea.

Keratoconus

This is a thinning of the cornea causing it to become cone-shaped and resulting in distorted vision; it is more common in older children and young adults.

Microphthalmia

This is when a baby is born with one or both eyes being unusually small. Find out more at **www.macs.org.uk**

Myopia (short sightedness)

Things are seen more clearly near to than in the distance; the opposite of hypermetropia. This is typically corrected by spectacles or contact lenses.

Nystagmus

This is an involuntary 'wobble' movement of the eyes from side to side or up and down, which results in an unclear image. Find out more at **www.nystagmusnet.org.uk.**

Optic atrophy

This is the deterioration of the optic nerve.

Retinitis pigmentosa

A group of hereditary diseases of the retina that sometimes result in 'tunnel vision', when there is a gradual loss of peripheral vision. Find out more at **www.brps.org.uk**

Retinoblastoma

This is a malignant tumour of the retina. This cancer only affects children under the age of five. It is very rare, but you can help: sometimes the flash from a camera can cause the pupil's eye to look white rather than red when you see the photo. This can be a sign of something serious, so suggest to the parent that they consult their GP. Over 95 percent of children will survive after treatment. Find out more at **www.chect.org.uk**.

Retinopathy of prematurity

This describes the damage to the retina in a premature baby's eye.

Strabismus (squint)

This is sometimes called an eye 'turn' where both eyes point in different directions due to a muscle imbalance or long sight: one eye looks at the object, but the other looks elsewhere. This is a very common condition in childhood. It is estimated that around 5 percent of children have some kind of strabismus. A squint is often first noticed when a child starts to focus on close objects, usually around the age of two or three, possibly when they start at an Early Years setting. Children do not outgrow a squint so an early eye examination is highly recommended. If a child has a squint, the brain ignores the image from the squinting eye. Over time, this can result in amblyopia or a 'lazy eye' (see earlier). If treatment is not made available, the lazy eye will remain permanently weak and the vision will not improve. The treatment may include prescribing glasses for a child, or encouraging them to wear an eye patch. This is put over a child's good eye to make the weaker eye work harder. The orthoptist (see page 25) will recommend how long each day it is to be worn, and for how many weeks or months. It can sometimes be hard to encourage a child to wear the patch, so try to do it when they are involved in something they enjoy and not when they are moving around a lot. Remember that they will be like a child with a visual impairment while they are wearing the patch: they will not see as well as usual. You can find out more on **www.strabismus.org**.

Each visual condition, such as cataracts, strabismus or nystagmus for example, will affect vision in different ways, and the individual characteristics of each child mean that the way they use this vision will vary greatly.

If you have been given a diagnosis of the condition affecting a child's vision, you may like to find out more about it.

There are support groups for people who have particular eye conditions such as albinism, retinoblastoma, nystagmus or retinitis pigmentosa, and for their families. 'Contact a Family' is a national organisation offering support and advice to families of children with disabilities, whatever their medical condition. Their website, **www.cafamily.org.uk**, has an A–Z list of specific conditions and rare disorders, including all the main visual conditions (such as albinism, retinoblastoma, nystagmus or retinitis pigmentosa), a section on vision in childhood, and details of support groups. In addition, **www.viscotland.org.uk**, is a website with explanations of medical information about visual impairment written specifically for parents.

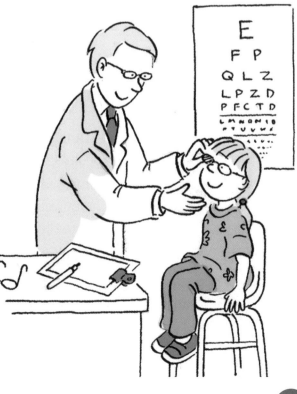

Some common myths

Here are some common myths about visual impairment. You may find that some of the children you work with will ask you questions like these, so your answers can help to dispel misunderstandings about visual impairment.

Myth: All blind people see nothing

Fact: Blind people do not all live in a world of complete darkness: only a few are totally blind and most of these can still distinguish between light and dark.

Myth: Blind people have a special gift

Fact: Blind people do not have a better sense of touch or hearing to compensate for their loss of vision. It takes practice and appropriate support to make good use of other senses.

Myth: Eating carrots will improve your vision

Fact: Carrots are high in Vitamin A, which is important for growth, eyesight and fighting infections. Eating carrots will not improve your vision but a balanced diet can help to prevent vision problems later in life.

Myth: Sitting close to the television will harm your eyes

Fact: There is no evidence that sitting close to the television will damage your eyes. Children should sit wherever they are most comfortable when watching TV.

Myth: Reading in dim light will damage your vision

Fact: Reading in low levels of light can make your eyes feel very tired, but it is not harmful and cannot permanently damage your vision.

Myth: It is not harmful to look at the sun if you wear dark glasses

Fact: The sun's ultraviolet light will still get to your eyes, damaging the cornea, lens and retina. You should never look directly at the sun or a solar eclipse.

Myth: You can wear out your eyes by using them too much

Fact: Babies and young children need to use their vision to develop it. Cutting down on reading or close work will not help or harm your eyes.

Myth: All people with a visual impairment wear glasses

Fact: Glasses cannot correct all visual impairments. They only help some people with particular eye conditions and if your glasses fully correct your vision, you are not visually impaired. Wearing glasses does not make your eyes lazy.

Early identification of a visual impairment

What to look for

As an Early Years practitioner, your observations will provide information on how a child is using their vision. The following may be indications of a visual impairment:

- inflamed, cloudy, bloodshot or weepy eyes
- drooping or swollen eyelids
- squints of any kind in one or both eyes
- unusual eye movements, such as flicking or wobbling
- blinking, rubbing or screwing up of eyes
- discomfort in bright light or in the dark
- moving head rather than eyes while reading
- unusual (very long or very short) viewing distance, such as when watching television
- poor body posture when working at a table
- unusual head posture when concentrating on a task
- complaints of dizziness, headaches or general eye discomfort
- poor eye contact
- clumsy movements and poor balance
- bumping into objects at the side or on the ground
- difficulty with stairs and steps
- reluctance to join in activities outside
- not answering unless addressed by name
- closing or covering one eye
- poor attention or concentration span
- difficulties with hand-eye co-ordination activities
- errors in reading and writing, especially if good orally.

Whilst many of these symptoms will be present in children with no eye problems, it is important to realise that they may be an indication of impaired or fluctuating vision, so it is always advisable to suggest to parents that they take their child for an eye test. Annual eye tests are advisable for all children, even very young children. The tests are free and help is available towards the cost of lenses and frames.

The National Screening Committee recommends that all children should be screened locally for visual impairment between the ages of four and five. It is a good idea to check with parents that this has been done.

If you suspect that a child may have a visual impairment, then it is essential that it is investigated. The first action is to discuss this with the parents/carers. As much information as possible should be gathered from parents and from medical sources, with parental permission, as well as by observation. Your setting SENCO or Area SENCO may also be able to offer advice (see page 26).

Various aspects of vision can be measured, and children do not need to be able to read or communicate clearly for an assessment to be made: near and distance vision can be tested to assess how clearly a child can see fine detail (visual acuity); colour discrimination, visual fields (what is visible around us at any one moment), effect of lighting, adaptation to dark and movement perception can also be assessed.

The measurement of the correct lenses needed to bring the images seen by the eyes into best focus is known as refraction. Children with reduced vision should be refracted to check whether they would benefit from glasses. Not all children with a visual impairment will need glasses, but early diagnosis and correction of refractive errors is very important in young children. A blurred image on the developing retina can lead to vision failing to develop properly or loss of vision in one eye.

You need to know whether a child should wear glasses, contact lenses or an eye patch and, if so, when and for how long. It is also important to know how much and how far a child can see and the best working conditions to enable them to play and explore successfully. For example, colour contrast and lighting may be especially important.

Not all children like wearing their glasses! Some may just not like the feel of the glasses on their face, or they may find the clearer world they are seeing through their glasses too different from the image they are used to. The first thing is to make sure that the glasses are comfortable and fit well. Some children may wear glasses with curl sides or with stretchy bands to help to keep them in place. Try to encourage the child to wear their glasses for activities that they enjoy. Keep the activity short, then build it up gradually. This could take weeks or months!

Certificate of Vision Impairment

The information gathered about a child's vision may be used to issue a Certificate of Vision Impairment. This is signed by a consultant ophthalmologist (see below) to register someone as sight impaired/partially sighted or severely sight impaired/blind. Very young children may not have a certificate until they are older. Some parents are anxious that it may 'label' their child, but feedback from families does not suggest that this is a problem. Although registration has no necessary connection with the assessment of educational needs, it does help to collect information about the numbers and causes of severe sight problems to help with planning services for children. It also helps to secure entitlement to benefits, such as Disability Living Allowance. A parent may want to talk this through with an ophthalmologist when they are ready.

Who can help?

Eye specialists

The **family doctor** (or GP) is concerned with the general health of a child and can advise and arrange further examinations with eye specialists.

Ophthalmologists are specialist doctors based at the hospital. They have special qualifications and experience in eye disorders, and in treating them with appropriate medicine and surgery. A child may be referred to one to check that their eyes are healthy.

The **orthoptist** usually works with the ophthalmologist at the hospital, but may be in a health clinic or visiting a school. They will test a child's sight, look at eye movements, assess how well both eyes work together and check for squints (turning eyes).

The **optometrist or ophthalmic optician** specialises in measuring a child's sight and may prescribe glasses. They can identify eye diseases and are based in a hospital or optician's. The dispensing optician will help to choose frames and make sure they fit properly, but cannot test a child's sight or prescribe glasses. It is important that if a child needs glasses, they are encouraged to wear them.

Your local authority should have at least one **Qualified Teacher of Visual Impairment** (QTVI) to work with you and the child in the setting. These specialists are qualified teachers who have additional qualifications and experience in working with children with a visual impairment. If you have difficulty getting help, or need the details of the specialist teacher in your area, contact the RNIB Helpline (see organisations on page 59).

Other professionals who can help

Your setting will have a **Special Educational Needs Co-ordinator** (or SENCO). Their role is to record and document the special educational needs processes in the setting, liaise and work with parents, help you find training if you need it, and liaise with outside agencies such as the QTVI. The local authority may have an **Area SENCO** who works with non-maintained settings to support young children with special educational needs. They may be part of the Early Years Inclusion Team and may be called an **Early Years Support Teacher**. The aim of the Area SENCO is to support the work of the setting-based SENCO and promote inclusion in Early Years settings.

The **Portage Worker** may also be part of the Early Years Inclusion Team. Portage is a home-based teaching service for children in the Early Years who have complex special educational needs. The Portage service supports parents teaching their children new skills.

The **Specialist Health Visitor** is a qualified nurse and health visitor with additional experience, knowledge and skills relating to childhood disability and its impact on the child and family. They provide a link between the range of health services a child and family may receive.

Implications: what does this mean for learning?

Children who have a visual impairment develop much the same as any child, although there may be differences in the rate and sequence that they develop skills.

Possible barriers to learning

Lowenfeld (1974) identified three main barriers to learning for children with visual impairments:

- Restrictions in the range and variety of experiences: children with a visual impairment are likely to experience fewer incidental learning opportunities than sighted children because they do not observe so much of what is going on around them.

- Restrictions in the ability to get about: the more severe their visual difficulty, the less independent children are likely to be in moving around. (This in turn leads to the third point.)

- Restrictions in interactions with the environment: visual impairment can reduce the ability of a child to experience and manage different aspects of their environment.

General implications

- A child's **level of vision may vary** from day to day, or even moment to moment. Their vision may be dependent upon their surroundings, as lighting can vary considerably from place to place. Even mood can affect a child's ability to see and make sense of the indistinct picture that the brain is receiving. If a child is feeling tired, unwell or is under any pressure, they may not be able to use their vision as well as usual.

- A child with any degree of visual impairment may not have the same **range and variety of real-life experiences**, such as active participation in the daily routines of eating, bathing and dressing which lead to independence. They may be less sure of their ability to get about, which will affect their interaction with the physical environment.

- Both the **quality and the quantity of the information** available for a child who has visual impairment may be decreased. They may not have the benefit of vision to understand the meaning of sounds or the function of objects. The child may perceive only part of an object or activity. Fragmentation of experiences is much more likely to occur with low levels of vision or absence of vision. The result is that the child's development may take place more slowly and unevenly than you expect, with possible gaps in their understanding.

- **Generalisation of concepts** is more difficult due to this fragmentation and different perceptions. This has significant implications for the time required to fully appreciate generalised concepts. For example, a child with full vision can see at a glance the relationship between a set of the same objects, such as a tray of different sorts of cups. A child who has a significant visual impairment and who has to use touch and hearing, or touch, hearing and low vision to explore each object, will take longer to make the same connection.

- **Imitation** is a key learning skill. Children who have limited vision or no vision will be significantly disadvantaged in their opportunities and ability to imitate visually.

- Vision supports **incidental learning**. Many skills that children may be expected to 'pick up' must be introduced directly to children who have a visual impairment as they have reduced opportunities to learn incidentally like their fully sighted friends.

- It may take a child **more time** to complete activities that involve using vision. This can be frustrating for you and for them; the extra time and extra effort that it takes to do everyday things can also make them more tired.

- **Our distance senses** – hearing and vision – allow us to **anticipate** what may happen next: if we touch a child who cannot see without giving them warning through speaking to them first, they may react badly.

There is a danger in concentrating on the practical effects of a visual impairment in terms of accessing information. Understanding the effects on communication, self-esteem and attitudes to learning are important to support a child's whole development. This is particularly significant for their relationships with other children and adults as, eye contact, facial expressions, body language and gesture may go unnoticed or be misinterpreted.

A child's responses will vary depending on the extent to which they adapt and compensate for a visual impairment by using and interpreting information from other senses with which they learn.

The effect of visual impairment and complex needs for learning

Children with a visual impairment and other complex needs will have a wide range of individual needs. A child may have reduced hearing, touch sensitivity, hand function and mobility in addition to difficulties in processing information and understanding concepts. Vision plays such a significant role in the co-ordination of information and learning that any impairment of vision in children with complex needs should be considered in terms of having a multiplying influence, rather than being considered simply as an additional area of need.

This may lead to reduced access to learning activities and the physical and sensory environment, and inhibit interaction with adults and other children. The child's motivation and ability to explore, initiate and take part in activities may also be affected. Consequently, adult expectations may be lower and the child's dependence and passivity may be increased. A particular challenge is to find ways to enable children who have a visual impairment and complex needs to become active participants in their own learning process.

Guiding themes

The EYFS outlines four themes to guide the work of adults working with young children. These focus attention on the key approaches to learning for children with a visual impairment.

A unique child

'Every child is a competent learner from birth who can be resilient, capable, confident and self-assured'.

Remember that normality to a child is what 'I am', so they will think that what they see is normal and the same as what everyone else sees. Children may be unaware that they see in a different way and may not have the language to describe what and how they see. By your observations, and with the support of your local advisory teacher of visual impairment, you can support each child by understanding how they make sense of the world: by encouraging them to use all their senses to imitate and copy, by giving them extra time to complete activities, and by giving them cues so that they can anticipate what will be happening next so that they begin to feel confident and in control. And remember, the sighted children will pick up on a lot from how you model interaction with a child with a visual impairment.

Positive relationships

'Children learn to be strong and independent from a base of loving and secure relationships with parents and/or a key person'.

You are the most important resource for a child with visual impairment. The way you interact with a child will support them in developing independence.

You can help by using the correct language with a child –

- commenting: putting into words the events and experiences that are happening

- connecting: pointing out links and providing structure

- creating: creating opportunities to maximise social interaction
  For more information about this case study see www.rnib.org.uk/learning
  http://www.rnib.org.uk/xpedio/groups/public/documents/PublicWebsite/public_ccinc.hcsp

Try to place your language on a child's action, not the other way round, so that you make the connection, with what they are showing interest in, to help them to develop the concept. For example, if they glance at a book or find it by touch, you can reinforce this by naming it as a book. This may need repeating many times before a child is confident to use the word and have a sense of 'bookness'.

If you need to guide a child's hand, try not to cover their hand with yours or move it for them; it gives a child more sense of control if you place an object under a child's hand to encourage them to explore it, or place your hand under theirs to demonstrate an action so that they can feel the movement but can withdraw if they feel at all anxious.

Enabling environments

'The environment plays a key role in supporting and extending children's development and learning'.

You can think about the environment like ripples on a pond: starting from the space that a child is immediately in touch with – their personal space – then the indoor space that is the room where they play, and on into the outdoor space which is all around. A child needs to feel confident to reach out from their personal space, to the wider world indoors and outdoors. They may need time to take in things around them, such as the sounds they hear, before they start to explore gradually and make choices about what they would like to do.

In all areas of the environment – walls and windows, furniture and floors – try to make sure that there is clarity and contrast, and avoid glare. You may also need to check what kind of lighting will suit a child: brighter is not always better for all children. Make sure that the touch and sound environment is meaningful and engaging for a child. It is useful to sit in a room with your eyes closed to find out what the sounds mean to you. Are they distracting or helpful?

You can use these questions to help:

- Is the natural light coming into the room controllable by blinds or curtains?

- Is there glare from windows or on surfaces, such as the tables?

- What kind of electrical lighting is provided e.g. strip or spot? Can this be controlled?

- Are there useful auditory clues, such as constant sounds like a bubbling fish tank, to help a child to locate where they are?

- Does the noise level in the room prevent a child from hearing other environmental sounds?

- Is all equipment and storage kept in the same place and clearly labelled with pictures, print and braille?

- Are displays at a child's height?

- Are there different floor surfaces to give different sound and touch feedback?

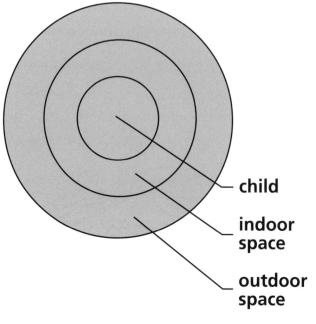

child

indoor space

outdoor space

- Is the flooring plain and not patterned?

- Are areas clearly defined, such as the home corner and the computer corner?

- Does furniture contrast clearly with the walls and floor?

- Are edges of steps highlighted?

- Are obstacles and clutter kept to a minimum?

- Are changes to the environment kept to a minimum?

Learning and development

'Children develop and learn in different ways and at different rates, and all areas of learning and development are equally important and interconnected.'

All children learn actively through play. They need:

- play partners – who can tune in to their play

- play space – which is responsive to their play

- play time – which goes at the pace they want

- play things – which are meaningful.

'Little steps to Learning' (see 'Further reading') suggests some factors to take into account when choosing play materials:

W – weight

E – ends and edges

S – size, shape and sound

T – texture and temperature.

Using treasure baskets (see 'Early Years factsheets' in Further reading page 63) can be a good way of making sure that you can take WEST into account so that children have a rich variety of experiences when they explore different objects.

Stages in development

Let's consider some of the key areas for early development.

Early exploration

Learning through the senses and movement is a recurring theme in early childhood. All human communication requires some form of movement. Children are motivated to make voluntary movements when they are interested in things beyond their own body and when they understand that they can reach and obtain these things even when they are not in direct contact with them.

Social interaction

Babies are born into a social world. Through interacting with others, they learn about who they are, about their own feelings and how to behave. As they grow, they learn more about other people's feelings. Adults are important for children, especially when giving sufficient and sensitive support to help a child achieve something successfully, without taking control, letting the child take the lead.

Shared discovery/joint attention

Adults support young children's learning through shared discovery; they help them to discover an object or activity through joint attention, sharing an interest and learning together. This is a foundation for social development, play and learning, communication and language.

Meaning making

Much early learning about the social and physical world develops through incidental learning when children look at people and things. Introducing meaningful experiences to a child is very important to help them to build appropriate concepts of the social and physical world.

Play and learning

Play is one of the main ways that young children learn about their world. Babies learn through repeated experiences; they learn through their senses about their bodies, other people and the objects in their immediate world. They start to explore and experiment with objects. They also try out actions and learn from the feedback on their experiments.

The EYFS supports these aspects through overlapping stages of learning. Children will not necessarily progress sequentially through these stages, but the following gives some indication of what children might be interested in at each of these stages.

A baby with a visual impairment will develop in much the same way as other babies, although there will be some individual differences. Babies need to develop shared attention, a sense of other people, and of learning about the world through other people. There is a potential risk to early conversations involving eye contact between the baby and parent/carer: the parent may have difficulties tuning in to the child without the benefit of mutual gaze. There may also be an absence of pointing to and looking at an object by the baby. Babies and infants with visual impairments sometimes use vocalisations, body movements or even stilling instead, but this may be more difficult to interpret as it involves small changes, such as a pause in hand or feet movements or a quietening in breathing.

Babies need to spend time with people who encourage their play and so involve them in shared activities, such as action songs or rhymes. Explain or describe sounds so that they mean something to the child, and try to name the toys that are being played with. Exploring different objects with hands and mouth is the child's way of experimenting and finding out about the world. Introduce toys that respond to a child's actions and give them plenty of time to explore.

Encourage babies to play on their tummies. You can start with a baby over your lap, maybe with a mirror to look into, then encourage them to play on the floor on quilts with a range of toys or on a play mat. You can use cushions or rolls for a blind baby to support them in raising their head, and encourage them with a musical toy. 'A Little Room' is also a good way of presenting objects that the baby can reach for when on their tummy (see Lilli Nielsen's website in Useful websites page 60).
Babies may also need to be encouraged to move: sound-producing toys can be useful for giving the child the motivation to shuffle or crawl.

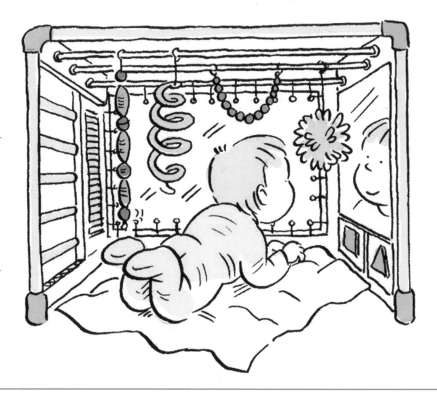

16 to 36 months

Children may enjoy mainly repetitive play, recapping real life; they need more repetitions of 'practice play' so that they can move on to symbolic, pretend play. There will be restricted opportunities for visual imitation, but this can be practised through verbal imitation of others. Children with a visual impairment will also be developing listening as a strategy for gaining information that sighted children can gain with a swift glance, so they may need to stop an activity in order to listen. It is important to encourage exploration of the physical environment as well as exploratory play so that the child can learn by discovery. Children with a visual impairment will need to experience lots of objects to make more connections and comparisons. Spoken language will remain the main means of communication and children will use language as a tool to aid action, talking themselves through activities. At this stage, structured activities may be more meaningful for a child.

Try to increase the child's skills in movement and in handling objects. Practise throwing, catching and kicking audible balls. Play with toys that come apart and fit together, and use objects to help with recognition of shapes and size. Encourage imaginative play to differentiate from real situations. Music is good for learning about different sounds and language. Read stories together and encourage mark making. Try to widen the child's circle of playmates in the setting.

30 to 60 months

It is important to have shared expectations for behaviour, but vision gives cues and a context for a child, such as advance warning of preparing for the next activity, so that a child can anticipate what is going to happen: if an adult puts on a coat, they could be going outside. Children will be developing supported independence or interdependence with other children and people. They will be developing an interest in semi-structured activities, such as construction building, where the frame of reference is set but the content of interaction is dependent on the spontaneous actions of other children.

However, they may still be having problems in free play: the types of toys may not be appropriate or they may have difficulties in following the play of other children because of the fast movement or non-verbal communication used. Symbolic play is often with adults or alone, not with other children.

Children are now building a stronger sense of their own identity and their place in the wider world. It is useful to further extend their social, independence and communication skills. Start to introduce the idea of rules for games and practise group games together. Encourage collaborative play, such as using construction materials, to encourage the child to play with other children. Dressing up is great fun for this age group. Use play to practise reading.

Areas of learning: implications and ideas

'Me do it!'

The call of toddlers 'me do it' reflects their burning desire to take control of their world, for example, doing up coat buttons, pouring a glass of milk or climbing stairs on their own. For a child with a visual impairment, this may be stated differently: they may say, for example, 'Carly do it', as they begin to work out who they are in relation to the world around them. The same message is still loud and clear.

Children from birth to five years are learning to learn. They are setting down those rich foundations for lifelong learning and beginning to see themselves as capable, confident learners.

But they can only do this if we as adults support and extend their learning. Home is the first place where children practise becoming independent, in a familiar environment with their first carers. Links with settings continue this process in an environment that is initially unfamiliar, and embraces a wider range of adults and children.

This balance of independence and interdependence is necessary for us all in our daily lives, and changes with the context we are in: put me in a kitchen and I am happy to prepare a meal independently; put me in a garage and I will willingly depend on a more experienced person to help me mend my car!

Becoming independent is an essential part of growing up. As children develop, they learn that they are separate beings with a mind of their own, who can do things for themselves. For children who are blind or partially sighted, this process may take longer. Children with additional complex needs may need long-term support to achieve small steps to independence. These steps must be no less valued.

The following sections consider in turn each area of learning of the EYFS in relation to young children with a visual impairment.

Personal, social and emotional

- Dispositions and attitudes
- Self-confidence and self-esteem
- Making relationships
- Behaviour and self-control
- Self-care
- Sense of community

Mutual eye contact is the foundation of early parent/carer and child bonding. Reduced opportunity for eye contact can create two-way difficulties from birth. Parents and carers may feel discouraged at what they perceive as a lack of response and this can be a barrier to early close relationships. The early process of building peer relationships continues to develop through visual contact and underpins the child's personal, social and emotional development.

Facial expression, body language and gesture are important. These aspects of communication may not be available in the same way to children who have a visual impairment. Often, expressing emotions through gesture, and understanding other people's body language, needs to be explained and encouraged. Also, some children who have a visual impairment may develop unusual mannerisms that they are unaware of, such as rocking. Later, such difficulties may affect relationships with sighted friends, whose visual signals are not seen by the child with sight problems. Or vice versa, sighted friends may misinterpret signals from a child with a visual impairment.

Typically, a sense of self as distinct from others is established mainly through vision. Developing body image is an aspect of this self-concept. In sighted people, vision plays a major part in the development of a self-image and enables us to see the effect of our actions and the actions of others.

Consider Sophie: she is sitting at a table in the nursery fitting pieces into a puzzle. She has to get very close to the puzzle to be able to see it clearly, which means that she is not able to respond to the other children who are sitting near her, doing their own puzzles. They can look around at their friends at the same time as fitting pieces into their puzzles, so the activity is an opportunity for social learning too. For Sophie, the puzzle needs her full attention.

Daily routines can be a rich source of learning for children; they are not just the unavoidable tasks of personal care to keep children clean, well fed and clothed. They are a rich point of interaction between the child, the environment and the adult, a focus for shared communication. But to make the most of this opportunity, routines need to be allocated time. It is far quicker when we are running late to do up those coat buttons for the child, but how does this support the child to do things for themselves and become independent? In this way, the daily routines of eating, dressing and using the toilet underpin the most important daily routine of all – social communication.

Here is a list of things to consider:

- A child with a visual impairment may need to sit in a specific position to be able to see what is going on. This is normally at the front of the group near the adult, but may be to one side depending on the child's eye condition. This will need careful planning if children are not to be separated from their friends, who may want to sit elsewhere.

- Try not to do something for the child that they are able to do independently – even if time is pressing – and encourage the other children not to 'baby' a child with a visual impairment. Your expectations of the child will be picked up by other children.

- If necessary, break down tasks into smaller steps so that the child can complete them successfully and gradually build up to the whole activity. For example, put the zip on a coat together for the child, but encourage them to pull it up.

- Children with a visual impairment usually take longer to do things. Allow extra time so that they have the satisfaction of completing an activity.

- Adults can help by giving extra explanations of social situations, such as 'Can you hear Anna crying outside? She is upset because she bumped into the climbing frame and hurt her shoulder.'

- Some social skills will need to be taught specifically: for instance, if a child is finding it hard to make friends, you may need to set up a situation, such as taking round the fruit at break to encourage them to approach other children. Or you may need to help them to locate a friend outdoors if they cannot see detail at a distance. You can model useful phrases in social situations: 'Let's find Terry and ask him if we can join in playing with the blocks.'

- You can set up shared experiences so that a child with a visual impairment is able to contribute within a group. Try a wheeled toy that one can ride while the other pushes, water play where turn taking can take place, or a basket of musical instruments to share. You may need to check the roles assigned to individual children, for instance in role play, so that the child with a visual impairment is not always the baby or the patient!

- Try to combine a sound cue, like a tambourine, with a physical action like raising a hand as a signal to the class that you want them to be quiet so that all the children can respond to the same cue.

- If the other children ask you a question about a child with a visual impairment, such as 'Why do Sammy's eyes wobble?', redirect the question to the child and help with the answer if needed. For instance, you could say, 'Sammy, can you tell Jane why your eyes wobble?' They may respond with, 'I can't see clear because they don't work properly.'

- Attach rings to zips to make them easier to grip; and a ring attached to a towel, apron or coat will make it easier to hang up on the hook.

- Make high-frequency events, such as toileting and dressing, an opportunity for social play.

- When feeding, talk and describe everything you are doing, as a child may not anticipate the food arriving in their mouth. Let a child get their hands in the food first – it can be messy, but will help them to understand the textures and where the food is coming from.

- Some children with a visual impairment are put off by 'sloppy' food. You can try 'dips' as a way of introducing soft food. Some children do not like lumpy food, so build up gradually from puréed food to solids.

- Most importantly, the child should have a key person to ensure consistency and continuity.

Communication, language and literacy

- Language for communication
- Language for thinking
- Linking sounds and letters
- Reading
- Writing
- Handwriting

Learning to communicate is vital for all development, to allow a child to have choice and control, and to form relationships. A great deal of teaching and learning takes place through the spoken word. Although children with little or no vision may use words appropriately, they may give a slightly different meaning to them. The meaning may be based on their individual experiences gained through limited vision, or their auditory or tactile experiences. Equally, they may understand the language used by adults and other children in an individual way. Visual language, such as the language of colour, is an obvious area of potential misunderstanding, but not the only one. However, do not be anxious about naming colours with a blind child: it is important vocabulary for them to learn.

Some aspects of communication depend on being able to see clearly: facial expressions and body language need to be seen in order to interpret the mood or meaning of another person. Vision also helps us to give attention to an object that becomes the focus of a shared meaning between the adult and child, or the child and other children.

Here is a list of things to consider:

- It is fine to use phrases like 'Let's look at the rabbits' or 'We're going to watch the DVD'. Keep your language as natural as you can to provide good examples.

- Always address a child by name as you approach, and say who you are. Don't forget to say when you are going away!

- Children with a visual impairment will need to use appropriate materials, such as books. Most children will benefit from clearly contrasted materials, and may have trouble with books where the print merges with the illustrations. Provide books with clear print and pictures. Textured books with flaps or levers will also help to hold the child's attention, and avoid laminating so as to reduce glare from the page.

- Specialist teachers of visual impairment will give advice on the use of enlarged or tactile materials.

- If the child has special resources, such as reading stands, magnifiers, large print books or coloured paper, these should be available alongside everyone else's materials.

- You can help in interpreting non-verbal communication, such as body language and facial expressions, by explaining 'Dan has crossed his arms and is frowning: he is angry that he cannot play with Sarah.'

- Some blind children use talk to keep themselves in contact with other people. Encourage them to keep their talk related to the activity that they are engaged in.

- You may need to draw a child's attention to the print that is around them so make sure that print on labels, signs and posters is large enough to see. The specialist teacher will advise on having braille in the environment for blind children.

- Provide chunky felt tips or thick soft pencils that make a good contrast with the paper so that a child can see their mark making.

- Some children have trouble building concepts. They need lots of hands-on experiences and explanation to understand that a word like 'cup' refers to all cups, not just to their cup.

- Provide extra explanations of words like jungles, dragons, rainbows and pirates, which feature in children's stories, but which could be outside a child's direct experience.

- Wherever possible, use real objects to help to explain what you are talking about, or to illustrate stories, and give children time to explore them. If you are using a toy, make this clear, such as 'Tom is showing you his toy dog'. This will be very different from the warm noisy dog that they may have at home!

- Give children time to preview and review new stories: share the book with them first so that they gain an understanding of the story – but leave out the last page so that they still get the excitement of waiting for the ending along with the rest of the group! Then go over the story again later to check understanding.

- Numbers as labels and for counting

- Calculating

- Shape, space and measures

A great deal of a child's mathematical understanding comes through handling real objects and through language. These are both areas in which a child with a visual impairment can participate and learn, with plenty of opportunity for concrete learning, especially outdoors and in daily routines.

It is important to encourage problem solving across all the areas of learning so that the child becomes an active learner, asking questions and seeking answers. It will also help a child with a visual impairment to make connections across areas of learning.

Here is a list of things to consider:

- Make sure that objects for counting are viewed against a contrasting background to make them easier to find. If necessary, when counting or sorting, use a tray or other container to keep the objects being counted in place. Encourage a child to work systematically so that they know which items have been counted and which still need to be counted.

- Use stories, songs and action rhymes so that numbers become meaningful in a range of contexts.

- A child may not be able to see the numbers that are all around in the environment – on the door, street signs, on the telephone and on the walls. Draw attention to them and let the child trace over the shapes with a finger.

- Measuring is about comparing sizes and quantities. A child will learn much through repeated practical activities, like sand and water play. Talk about containers that are too big or too small.

- Try to give the child opportunities to handle real money rather than plastic coins.

- Talk about the shape of everyday things that are familiar to the child – a rectangular door, a circular table or a triangular cheese! Encourage them to feel similar shapes of different sizes to help to make comparisons between big and small objects, and use these terms accurately.

- Exploration and investigation

- Designing and making

- ICT (Information and Communication Technology)

- Time

- Place

- Communities

A child with a visual impairment is likely to have gaps in general knowledge due to limited or fragmented experiences as a result of their reduced vision. Chances to learn incidentally will also have been reduced, so a child may not know the name of a simple, basic object because they did not see what people were referring to when it was named and therefore cannot connect the two.

A lot of opportunities to experience real-life objects in real-life situations will help a child to start making these connections, linking the name to the object, such as a cup, and so developing a concept of 'cupness'. The more severe the visual impairment, the more important this becomes.

Here is a list of things to consider:

- Care needs to be taken to ensure that any gaps in knowledge are identified by specific questioning, such as 'What would happen if…?' and by encouraging the child to ask questions too.

- When showing a child how to use tools, give guidance from behind so that the child may see or feel the adult's hands in the correct position.

- Time is a difficult concept for a child who may never have seen a clock. Give lots of opportunities to talk about the past and how things change.

- Try to give structure to the day by talking about landmark times in sequence, for example, when the child eats, returns home and goes to bed.

Computers will be increasingly important for children with a visual impairment as they move through their education, so try to introduce aspects of ICT into their everyday world in a meaningful way through play. This can be low tech, such as mobile phones or calculators, but here is one high tech idea from a practitioner on the use of a plasma screen:

'It has a 52" touch screen, and is very mobile and height adjustable. I have been using PowerPoint to make short interactive stories to use in group sessions. This appears to be a good way of introducing IT to the children. They cannot only be used with the touch screen but also with switches and can be tailored to suit an individual's needs, such as by changing the background colour, and setting the speed and size of the animations. I have recently made one for November 5th, making shapes and sounds to represent fireworks. Another one I have made is the "Mrs Mopple's washing line" story, with washing flying off the washing line and landing on the animals. This way of using the screen makes story time accessible to all the children, which we also back up with props and an activity to go along with the theme, making the whole session more inclusive. I have made many others and this form of communication is also useful on laptops in settings or in the home.'

The ICT section in the Early Years Foundation Stage recommends:

- For children from birth to 11 months – that they 'show interest in toys and resources that incorporate technology'.

- For children from 8 to 20 months – that they 'explore things with interest and sometimes press parts or lift flaps to achieve effects such as sounds, movements or new images'.

- For children from 16 to 26 months – that they 'show interest in toys with buttons or flaps and simple mechanisms, and begin to learn to operate them'.

- For children from 22 to 36 months – that they 'show an interest in ICT and seek to acquire basic skills in turning on and operating some ICT equipment'.

- For children from 30 to 50 months – that they 'know how to operate simple equipment'.

- For children from 40 to 60+ months – that they 'complete a simple programme on a computer; use ICT to perform simple functions, such as selecting a channel on the TV remote control; use a mouse and keyboard to interact with age-appropriate computer software, so that by the end of the Early Years Foundation Stage, they are ready to 'find out about and identify the uses of everyday technology and use information and communications technology and programmable toys to support their learning'.

Anyone who has watched a toddler trying to post a jam sandwich into the video player will know the interest young children have in ICT!

Most older school children use computers regularly to find information online, learn to use databases and type up their work to present it attractively using graphics and images from the internet. Most also enjoy playing computer games, downloading music and films, and keeping in touch with friends via social networking sites. Blind and partially sighted children have all these aspirations and can learn to use computers to give them access to print, braille and audio, and magnified text and images. So a positive attitude to ICT is an important foundation.

All word processing software on a computer can increase or decrease the size of print, and change the font and colour of the text if needed. To provide maximum contrast, if black on white is not suitable, paper in a range of colours may be used. A child can therefore have print of almost any size, font and colour on paper of almost any colour. Other software can be used to thicken lines for diagrams to make the outlines clearer.

Options within accessibility features on most computers allow the customisation of screens. For instance, in Windows, if you follow Start – Programs – Accessories – Accessibility – Accessibility Wizard, you can choose how to display colour settings, text and icon size, the size and colour of the mouse cursor and magnify sections of the screen.

ICT plays a major role in providing tools for children who have a visual impairment and complex needs, and enables them to interact with their environment, to indicate their choices and to display their knowledge. It gives opportunities to learners at all levels, from the very first toy that vibrates when a child hits it, or when a child makes a loud sound near it, right through to laptops with voice recognition input and braille software.

Using ICT can lead to an understanding of control, to an opportunity to choose and to a decision of whether or not to activate the toy. Having control over such equipment can lead to experiences that are fun and satisfying, and can contribute to self-esteem. For instance, battery-operated toys can be adapted for switch use: an adaptor lead can be attached with a simple single switch to encourage a child to operate a sound- or light-producing toy. You can find out more at **www.inclusive.co.uk**.

The value of the computer for visual stimulation was identified very early on, and there are many programmes that are designed to give practice in tracking skills, hand/eye co-ordination, object/colour recognition and matching. They also help to examine concepts such as size, colour, shape, odd-one-out and the same or different.

There are lots of programmes that are suitable for young children with a visual impairment. For example, **www.bbc.co.uk/cbeebies** has programmes that are suitable for blind and partially sighted children, and **www.inclusive.co.uk** has a range of programmes to encourage early looking. 'Leaps and Bounds' is just one that lots of practitioners recommend. 'Leaps and Bounds' has activities to introduce children in the Early Years to vital skills, including mouse skills, decision making, visual and auditory stimulation, left/right orientation and tracking. There are lots of ideas on **www.foundation.e2bn.org** too.

Touch monitors allow feedback from visual tasks to be registered directly onto the screen, and there are many different 'mice' that enable young children of all abilities to have direct action on the screen. Roller balls have given access to some children for whom the operation of the mouse would be too difficult, and switch accessible software is now commonplace.

However, it is not always necessary for children to sit in front of a computer to promote their use of ICT skills. You can provide a broad range of technology, such as digital cameras (blind children can be fascinated by these too), DVD players and electronic keyboards. Or children can make their own laptop, photocopier, cashpoint machine or barcode scanner to incorporate into their play. This will help them begin to understand the role of ICT in the world, to learn about the real world and explore it in their play.

Getting too close to a computer screen or TV cannot damage a child's eyes. The key thing to remember is that we do not inflict visual or auditory overload on young children through ICT, but that ICT is part of a well-balanced lifestyle where play with natural materials and objects indoors and outdoors is equally valued.

- Movement and space

- Health and bodily awareness

- Using equipment and materials

Seeing something motivates a child to want to find out what it is like. A child who is blind or who has a severe visual impairment often has diminished motivation to move, simply because not as many objects or experiences come to their attention.

Spatial awareness may also be delayed as there is not the same opportunity to demonstrate and observe basic concepts, such as in front, back, above, below etc.

Orientation may pose difficulties for some children. It takes time to build up a mental map of the surroundings through available vision and other senses. New environments often pose significant challenges and the consequences of bumping into things or falling are startling and sometimes painful, possibly resulting in anxiety for the child and a reluctance to explore.

But racing and chasing is part of every child's play. A child with a visual impairment may need adult support to learn how to look for, listen to, and find other children, but a well-planned environment can support the child in moving around more confidently and to be independent.

Here is a list of things to consider:

- Pegs and trays should be clearly labelled in a way that the child can access – with pictures, words, objects and braille. The child will have a better chance of finding things independently if they are clearly labelled, and the child has been shown specifically where to look for it.

- Clearly visible materials (with displays at the child's eye height), appropriate lighting levels (including blinds on windows to cut down on glare), and good visual contrast (such as highlighted edges to steps) can also help.

- Landmarks need to be established, for instance wind chimes, to help the child understand the layout of the setting. Through them, the child can learn routes, find playmates and look for an adult.

- A child with a visual impairment may be less confident outdoors so show them where the boundaries of the play area are: 'walk and talk' the child around the area.

- Let the child hold your finger, wrist or forearm when needed (rather than you holding their hand) as this gives the child more control.

- Obstacles, such as pillars in the middle of a play area, should be marked or highlighted. This increases visual contrast and ensures safety. The positioning of movable objects, such as small water and sand trays, needs to be carefully considered so they are not a hazard.

- A child also uses the sense of touch through their feet to identify walking surfaces. Point out edges of carpet and mats, sides of paths and the grass.

- Tactile markers may be used around the room to help a child to recognise which area they are in. Floor markers, for example mats, can be used to help a child to know where different play areas are: an elastic band just before the end of a hand rail to indicate that the steps are coming to an end or a raised picture on a door to show which room it is.

- Some settings paint a yellow line on the floor to mark key routes for a child, with instructions to the children and adults 'not to park on the yellow lines' so that they are kept clear!

- Try to keep the layout of a room consistent, but tell the child if there are any changes to the room or equipment.

- Games using boxes, tunnels and soft play areas involving the use of prepositions – up, down, in, over, on, through – will help when learning early mobility skills.

- It is easier for a child with a visual impairment to throw a ball than to catch it. This ability can be used in group games. Different coloured balls may be necessary to ensure good contrast against the floor or ground outside. Beanbags move slowly through the air and can make it easier for the child to track the movement when catching. Other interesting balls, with tails, knobbles or bells, are available from a variety of suppliers. Some children may need to be told when the ball is rolled or thrown so that they are ready to receive it.

- New physical activities may need to be demonstrated by an adult, as copying another child can be visually difficult. A child may also need some physical guidance as to how to move parts of the body.

- Being creative – responding to experiences – expressing and communicating ideas

- Exploring media and materials

- Creating music and dance

- Developing imagination and imaginative play

It is vital that all children are given opportunities to be creative. Some children with a visual impairment, particularly blind children, may be very literal and functional in their approaches and slower to develop imaginative play. They need longer to learn to do things for themselves, such as dressing and eating, before they begin to incorporate these actions into their play, such as dressing a doll and feeding it. Children who are blind or partially sighted can only role-play what they have experienced in life. As they may not see Dad shaving, Mum gardening or Grandma cooking, they will need hands-on ways of experiencing these activities before they can use them in pretend play.

Children with a visual impairment will not necessarily be more musical, but music does provide opportunities to practise listening, enjoy moving and playing with other children. The experience of painting is enjoyable even if the results cannot be seen, but some children with a visual impairment will be reluctant to get their hands messy or sticky as their hands are one of their best ways of getting information. They may need to be encouraged to explore different materials in a supportive way.

Here is a list of things to consider:

- You can help by providing a wide range of activities to which children can respond by using a range of senses: touching, hearing, smelling, tasting and seeing. Create opportunities for children with a visual impairment to explore different artefacts, materials, spaces and movements.

- Bold colours that contrast well will help most children. Textured paint (made by mixing paint with sand and glue) will provide tactile interest.

- The use of textured and shiny materials may enhance work such as collage, and coloured glue sticks, scented felt-tip pens and crayons all add to the learning experience.

- Give children opportunities before a music session to explore and experiment with the musical instruments, and to be near the teacher when demonstrations are taking place.

- If you are putting up a display in the setting, make sure that it is at the child's height so that they have the best opportunity to see it. Add objects or tactile parts for blind children to feel so that they can learn from the display.

Play plan

It is important that we record progress for children and think carefully about what might be the next step for them. One local authority visual impairment service has developed play plans for young children instead of IEPs (individual education plans). Here is one example:

April 2008

Name: Alice

DOB: 05.07.05

Progress so far:

Alice still enjoys exploring musical toys most of all, but also likes to make her own music with spoons or beads in a metal bowl. She enjoys singing nursery rhymes and other songs, for example, 'wind the bobbin up', and rocks to the music and makes some gestures. She can make choices as to which song she wants to sing, however, she is shy about doing these things in the nursery as yet.

Alice has a good number of words she uses and she holds quite long conversations, a lot of which are intelligible, although sometimes she seems to be talking to herself. She likes to play and receive attention, and gets frustrated if she doesn't get it but, at other times, she is resistant to being stimulated.

Things to try next:

Social and emotional development

- Alice enjoyed the pre-school trip to the farm and stroked several animals. She would benefit from further experience of different places for example, soft play areas, in order to broaden her experience of people and places.

- Sitting/standing with other children and encouraging them to speak to and touch Alice would be beneficial.

Communication, language and meaning

- Continue reading short stories to Alice and give her an object associated with the story, for example, a cat or toy van for Postman Pat.

- Encourage Alice to copy rhythms, tapping a drum or banging a spoon etc.

- Encourage Alice to make choices about which song to sing or which activity to try next.

Play and learning

- Ask Alice to find toys hidden under or in a cloth, tin or box.

- Challenge her to pull rings off a musical stack.

- Encourage Alice to play with toys of different textures, as well as sound-producing toys.

- Show Alice how to use fingers of both hands to explore objects, textures and parts of a toy, for example, a teddy's ears, parts of a tactile necklace made from metal nuts, beads and plastic reels etc.

Movement and mobility

- Encourage Alice to move along the sofa whilst standing, for example, to reach a favourite toy.

- Encourage standing to strengthen legs.

- Encourage bottom shuffling to reach a toy.

Towards independent self-care

- Encourage Alice to sit at a table to eat her meals.

- Encourage Alice to explore food with her hands.

- Tell Alice to pick up her own cup (with handles and spout) when she wants a drink.

Date for review: July 2008

Safety and risk management

All the usual safety considerations for young children apply, for example, guarding plugs, wires and hot radiators, supervising children on climbing frames and slides, and keeping doors onto the street shut. In addition, there are a few things that need extra thought when a child with impaired vision is part of the group.

Doors are a particular hazard because a blind or partially sighted child could walk into the edge of a half open door, or trap fingers in the hinge while feeling their way round. This can be avoided by keeping doors either wedged fully open or firmly shut.

Objects scattered about the floor are another hazard. To some extent, this is unavoidable and a blind child must learn to feel with hands and toes for obstacles. However, staff can be on the lookout for potential dangers, and all the children will benefit by learning not to leave toys about and to put them back after playing with them.

If a child wears glasses, standard plastic lenses are routinely supplied; these reduce the risk of breakage, but would not give protection from a blow to the face. There is no such thing as unbreakable or shatterproof lenses, so there may be some activities where a child will need to take their glasses off for safety or practical reasons, or when play is very boisterous or messy. It is a good idea to keep a second pair of glasses to hand in case the first set is damaged.

Some children will also wear contact lenses: these should be removed during sand play, if possible. You will need to discuss with the parent or guardian how these should be removed, cleaned and replaced.

If a child does need to take off their glasses or take out their lenses, they should know a safe place to store them, out of reach of other children, and where the child can find them again when needed. Children should also be encouraged to keep their glasses clean!

Working with families

When a child with a disability is born, the response from the parents and family is often complex, and their attitude may well change over time. The parents will often not know the nature or extent of the child's difficulties in the early days and, unless the child's eyes show obvious signs of damage, even a severe visual impairment may not be picked up and diagnosed for some months. This is even more likely if there are other difficulties present.

How parents react and cope varies from family to family: although childhood visual impairment may put pressure on family life, some families adapt positively and constructively, and believe that their lives have been enhanced by the experience. Others, however, may react with shock and disbelief. Whatever the reaction, parents say that when they hear that their child has a visual impairment, it is a moment that stays with them for the rest of their lives.

Parents also need to consider the effect that a child with a visual impairment may have on their sighted brothers and sisters. Possible adverse reactions of siblings may include the fact that they feel unable to compete or fight with their brother or sister; they may feel embarrassment in public, especially with their friends, or they may be over-protective. Another issue for some siblings is the extra time and attention that the child with a visual impairment may get from their parents.

Similarly, although close family members may come to a clear understanding of the visual impairment, it may be difficult to communicate this to friends and relatives.

Parents who have passed the condition on to their child, either knowingly or not, may carry feelings of guilt. Conversely, a blind or partially sighted parent who has a positive experience of visual impairment may take a very matter-of-fact approach to their child's disability and not regard the visual impairment as a particular issue.

Being a parent can be a complex and difficult role, one for which few of us receive training. Most people experience some difficulties while trying to become a competent parent! The added dimension of bringing up a child with a visual impairment means that at times parents may feel overwhelmed with the additional demands on their emotional and physical energy.

The EYFS recognises the key role that parents play in their children's education as a child's first and most enduring educator. When supporting parents, it is always wise to reflect carefully on the nature of your involvement and take into consideration the limits of your role. In essence, you need to reflect on the following questions:

- What is my role?
- How does it relate to the input of other professionals?
- What are the limits of my intervention?

Parental support may involve active listening, information sharing, exchanging thoughts and ideas, and offering reassurance. This may be through:

- a home-setting diary
- telephone calls
- informal discussions at the beginning and end of the day
- liaison between the parents and a range of other professionals
- home visits
- liaison in formal review meetings.

If you are a child's key person, you will have a great deal to contribute to any discussion regarding the child, working closely with any other professionals who may be involved.

The following may be useful to you in thinking about how you communicate with and support the families of children with whom you work:

- Take account of and respect the cultural and ethnic practices of different families when planning support.
- Use language and terminology that family members can understand.
- Be honest with parents about what you are able to do and be willing to admit if you make mistakes.
- Be open to learning from parents about their child.
- Respect privacy and confidentiality in your dealings with families.
- Do not stereotype families – get to know them as individuals.
- Do not assign blame to parents or say anything that could leave them feeling guilty.

Early support

The Early Support Programme is the central government mechanism for achieving better co-ordinated, family-focused services for young disabled children and their families across England.

The aim is well co-ordinated, multi-agency support that is family focused, flexible and which offers practical help underpinned by better information.

Despite the best efforts of many practitioners working with families, research into the needs of families of disabled children carried out at different times, in different areas of the country and on different populations, has delivered very consistent messages. Families have reported that they find it difficult to:

- find out about the services that are available to help them

- make sense of the role of different agencies and different professionals

- get professionals to understand their situation and needs in the context of the whole family

- have their own knowledge of their child recognised

- negotiate delays and bureaucracy.

The Early Support Programme promotes an integrated approach to family support services and has developed a range of materials to help those who work with families to co-ordinate their activity better and to work in partnership with parents. The programme materials include:

- a range of **Information for Parents booklets** on particular conditions or disabilities that provide standard 'first step' information for families, including one for visual impairment

- an **Early Support Family pack** containing a **Family file** that helps with service co-ordination on a day-to-day basis and provides background information about how services work

- an **Early Support Service audit tool** to help service providers and managers evaluate the quality of services being provided and plan for improvement

- a range of **developmental journals** that help families to track development in their child and which provide a common framework supporting discussion about the child over time, including one for visual impairment

- information on **informed choices** for families with a deaf child and for professionals working with them

- **Early Support professional guidance**, which introduces an Early Support approach to those who work with families and shows how the programme materials improve practice.

All local authorities are being encouraged to adopt an Early Support way of working to integrate services for families with young disabled children.

You can find out more on **www.earlysupport.org.uk**.

Transition

Going to an Early Years setting for the first time is a key stage for both child and parent. Children are primed to stay close to their parents so it is no surprise if, from the age of around eight months to three years, or older, children cry or protest when a parent leaves.

Visiting a setting allows a child to become familiar with the new surroundings and get to know other children and adults in the setting. This may take longer for a child with a visual impairment.

A key person system (one person who will take particular care of a child) is helpful. This person will form a special relationship with a child so that they build confidence and trust in the setting over time. In addition, try to build a child's confidence by:

- learning practical everyday tasks, such as dressing, eating and using the toilet

- talking to new adults, for example paying in a shop, so that a child is able to ask adults for help

- giving some responsibility, such as tidying toys, watering plants or feeding a pet.

When the parent starts leaving their child, build up the amount of time slowly. Try to encourage the parent not to play alongside their child, or they may think that their parent will always be there to play with them in the new setting. Aim, little by little, to distance the parent from their child, for example encourage the parent to wander to the edge of the room and talk to another parent so that the child can hear their voice and know that they are still there. Start by telling the child that their parent is going to another room for a couple of minutes and then will return. If the child is happy with that, gradually increase the time their parent is away. Tell the parent not to sneak off, even if the child is playing happily! Aim to build a 'goodbye' routine so that the child knows their parent is going, but is confident that they will always come back.

One way of helping a child to feel at home is to turn one area of the setting into a quiet corner. This can be created with available furniture with a removable entrance. It could enclose a child's favourite toys. The child can explore and feel secure in this area first and then the area can gradually be expanded. Other children can be invited to visit in ones or twos. As the child gradually wants to venture further into the play areas, the key person can help them to learn key routes and introduce them to all the activities on offer in the setting.

'Personal Communication Passports' or 'All About Me' booklets are a way of providing information on the important things about a child in an accessible and child-centred way. Some settings use the Early Support family file in this way. They build on parents' knowledge about their child and provide information on a child's special interests, personal care, eating preferences and ways of communicating, allowing a child to be understood when indicating choices or explaining their preferred way of looking at things, for instance if they need to get very close to books or the computer screen.

They are a good way of supporting children's transitions between settings, either from home to Early Years setting or between different types of setting, for example where a child may attend a nursery in the morning and childminder in the afternoon. They promote continuity of experiences for a child and help them to feel that the adults around them understand their needs, especially if they are new to the setting or visiting.

You can find out more on **www.communicationpassports.org.uk**.

You can help me by...

Don't forget, children may also have views on the setting they are in! These are some of the things a child might want to say to the adults and children in their setting:

Please remember...

- I would like to have the opportunity for the same experiences as everyone else, and for you to treat me like everyone else, with the same expectations, but:

  - I have to work harder on visual activities so I may get tired
  - I may see less well in bright or dim light
  - I may see less if I am worried or ill
  - I may not see body language
  - I may not see facial expressions.

Please help me by using...

- my name before giving me instructions

- the names of the other children so that I know who you are talking to

- curtains/blinds to control light from outside coming through the windows

- bright clear colours in resources and displays

- activities that use all the senses, such as touch and sound, as well as vision.

Please will you give me...

- posters/pictures/displays at my eye level that I can also touch

- individual demonstrations, such as actions for rhymes

- clear verbal instructions

- explanations for unexpected noises

- real objects to play with

- resources that are organised so that I can try activities on my own

- warning if routines are going to change in any way

- help to make friends.

Please let me...

- tilt my head if it helps me to see better

- go as close to things as I need to (this will not damage my eyes)

- have extra time for activities

NBCS

The National Blind Children's Society enables children and young people with visual impairments to achieve their educational and recreational goals. They provide educational advocacy advice, CustomEyes Books, ICT and sensory equipment, holidays and activities, family support and information.

www.nbcs.org.uk

Sense

Sense is the leading charity that supports and campaigns for children and adults who are deafblind. They have family, education and advisory services.

www.sense.org.uk

Useful websites

RNIB Parents' Place

A website for parents of blind and partially sighted children where they can pick up tips and advice, get information about RNIB's family events, support, health, rights and services, and talk to other parents on a message board.

www.rnib.org.uk/parents

RNIB Curriculum Clipboard

RNIB has a wealth of information for teachers and other professionals supporting the education of blind and partially sighted children and young people, including those with complex needs.

www.rnib.org.uk/curriculum

VI-forum

VI-forum is a UK-based email discussion group. It is intended primarily for teachers and teaching assistants to discuss issues and share information relating to the teaching of children with visual impairments.

http://lists.becta.org.uk/mailman/listinfo/vi-forum

Books for children on visual impairment

The books listed on this website may be of interest to anyone working with children, particularly children with physical or emotional problems. Browse the 'Sight' section for books about visual impairment.

www.healthybooks.org.uk

Wonderbaby

This is a website that is run by parents in America and has information on toys and equipment, including sensory rooms, and ideas for supporting blind babies and infants.

www.wonderbaby.org

RNIB Technology pages

RNIB's main site provides information on keyboard skills, computers, the internet and much more.

www.rnib.org.uk/technology

Inclusive Technology Ltd

A supplier of hardware equipment and software that helps people with special needs to use a computer, communicate and learn.

www.inclusive.co.uk

RNIB National Centre for Tactile Diagrams

Provides information and advice about all aspects of creating, teaching and supporting the use of tactile graphics.

www.nctd.org.uk

Ace Centre

A comprehensive site providing information on communication and technology for learners with complex needs. It includes a good explanation of Objects of Reference for children with visual impairment and complex needs.

www.ace-centre.org.uk

Moon Literacy

You can find out about teaching literacy and maths using Moon, research that is going on into Moon and access downloadable Moon font.

www.moonliteracy.org.uk

Widgit VI Symbols

Widgit have finished a two-year-long research project looking at how symbols can be made more appropriate for people with a visual impairment. The results from this are 2,400 modified symbols, based on the Widgit Literacy Symbols, and three extensive packs of resources.

www.widgit.com/products/vi

Intensive Interaction

Information on an approach to learning early communication for children and young people who have profound and complex needs. It is of particular relevance to those who are blind or partially sighted.

www.intensiveinteraction.co.uk

Personal Communication Passports

Guidance on the creation and use of passports. These are a practical and person-centred way of supporting children and young people who cannot easily speak for themselves.

www.communicationpassports.org.uk

Picture Exchange Communication System (PECS)

The site of Pyramid Educational Consultants, the originators and main source of information about the PECS system used with many children with learning difficulties, including those with partial sight.

www.pecs.com

MDVI Euronet
Information on European-wide work relating to the education of pupils who have visual impairment and multiple disabilities.
www.mdvi-euronet.org

Teaching Students with Visual and Multiple Impairments
Part of the website of The Texas School for the Blind. It contains a large number of articles on various aspects of teaching blind and partially sighted children with complex needs.
www.tsbvi.edu/Education/vmi/index.htm

Look Up
Information on eye care and vision for people with learning disabilities.
www.lookupinfo.org

Lea Hyvarinen
This homepage is created to share the teaching materials of Lea Hyvarinen, an ophthalmologist who is Senior Lecturer at the University of Helsinki, with other teachers in low vision, in vision screening and in occupational health.
www.lea-test.fi/leaweb

Lilli Nielsen
This homepage is for parents, therapists and educators who are interested in an 'active learning' approach that was developed by Lilli Nielsen, a Danish teacher and psychologist.
http://www.lilliworks.com/

Resources

BumpOns
A simple and effective way to mark everyday items. The raised bumps are supplied on self-adhesive sheets and are available in a range of sizes, shapes and colours.
www.rnib.org.uk/shop

Wikki stix
Endlessly re-usable flexible strips that can be bent, stuck together and pressed on to most surfaces to form creative and colourful tactile pictures. They are made from a non-toxic wax formula in a yarn strand. (Select 'Products' and enter 'Wikki' in the search box.)
www.rnib.org.uk/shop

Talking Tins
Originally designed for visually impaired people to identify different food tins, Talking Tins have lots of uses around the home or setting. Record a personal note or create a talking label for a toy box. Record a message of up to ten seconds and play it back at the touch of a button. (Select 'Products' and enter 'Talking tin' in the search box.)
www.rnib.org.uk/shop

Braille teaching materials
A range of teaching materials aimed at children learning braille, including reading packs for differing abilities, is available from RNIB's Online Shop. (Select 'Publications' and enter 'Braille' in the search box.)
www.rnib.org.uk/shop

Books for professionals

This keeps parents and professionals informed about RNIB books as well as titles of interest from other specialist publishers around the world. To keep up to date with recommended new titles and special offers, you can sign up for their free monthly eNewsletter.

(Select 'Publications' for your search.)

www.rnib.org.uk/booksforprofessionals

Count me in

An interactive training DVD produced by RNIB illustrating the principles and practices of effective inclusion in a range of educational settings. This resource is intended for anyone working with visually impaired learners, including class teachers, teaching assistants, special educational needs professionals and senior managers. "Count me in" consists of six separate films based on early years, mainstream and special school settings. These sections follow key themes such as attitudes and expectations, mobility and independence, access to the curriculum and communication skills. (Select 'Publications' for your search.)

2009, ED499, ISBN 9781858789989

www.rnib.org.uk/shop

Early Years factsheets

RNIB's Early Excellence Partnership Project has produced downloadable factsheets to help and guide both parents and professionals to encourage early development in children with sight problems. The factsheets include therapy sessions, infant massage, treasure baskets and information on sensory development resource boxes. (Select 'Publications' for your search.)

www.rnib.org.uk/learning for more information.

Early focus (Second edition) by Pogrund RL & Fazzi, DL

This is about working with young children with sight loss and their families. It provides a comprehensive overview of all the developmental areas that may be affected by vision loss. Four new chapters cover the delivery of early intervention services, developing skills in young children in areas of literacy, daily living, independence and motor behaviour.

2002, 532 pages, paperback, ISBN 9780891282150.

Available from American Foundation for the Blind, **www.afb.org**

Focus on foundation

Including children who are blind or partially sighted in Early Years settings. This second edition combines the ideas and expertise of many Early Years practitioners and qualified teachers of children with visual impairments. It is packed with practical ideas for the successful inclusion of children with sight loss for all who work in Early Years settings, including nurseries, reception classes, children's centres, playgroups and out of school clubs. It may also be of interest to childminders welcoming a child with sight problems into their home. For easy reference, it closely follows the format of the Early Years Foundation Stage and endorses the principles for Early Years learning and development. (Select 'Publications' for your search.)

2008, ED282, 68 pages, paperback, ISBN 9781858789170

www.rnib.org.uk/shop.

I'm posting the pebbles by Haughton, L and Mackevicius, S
This shows wonderful, creative ways for teachers and parents to interact with the different ways that children with sight loss learn. It is packed with ideas for teaching through play and addresses issues that tend not to arise with a fully sighted child. It also covers social interaction, orientation and mobility, routines, water, sensory play and literacy.
2001, 60 pages, paperback, ISBN 0949390585.
Available from Vision Australia (formerly Royal Victorian Institute for the Blind)
www.visionaustralia.org.au

Insight
This magazine for professionals working with children and young people, as well as for parents and carers, is published bimonthly. It focuses on the education, health and well-being of children with sight problems, including those with complex needs. Regular features include eye health, family life, early years, the curriculum and access to learning. For up-to-date subscription details, visit **www.rnib.org.uk/insightmagazine**.

Little steps to learning: play in the home for children who are blind or vision impaired, 0–3 years by Haughton, L & Mackevicius, S
This offers creative ways for families and teachers to interact through play with the unique learning needs of children who have a sight problem. It is packed with play ideas based on everyday activities and routines around the home and outside.
2004, 72 pages, paperback, ISBN 0949390615
Available from Vision Australia (formerly Royal Victorian Institute for the Blind)
www.visionaustralia.org.au

Playtime: toys and ideas for young children with sight loss (formerly Toy catalogue)
Produced with the British Toy and Hobby Association, this catalogue lists over 100 toys selected for their suitability for children with little or no sight. The toys are available in many high street shops and can be enjoyed by all children. Free of charge. (Select 'Publications' for your search.)
2008, PR10893 (Print) Available in other formats on request.
www.rnib.org.uk/shop

Play it my way
A resource book for parents providing a wealth of tried and tested play ideas, toys and materials that can be used to enliven everyday routines and help children with sight problems to find out about the world. (Select 'Publications' for your search.)
2000, ED130 (Print) ISBN 0117016764
www.rnib.org.uk/shop

Show me what my friends can see by Sonksen, P & Stiff, B
This describes the developmental difficulties babies and young children with sight problems may experience: emotional, language and speech, hand and localisation skills, as well as early concept formation. Ideas are suggested for how to overcome these difficulties and to promote the development and use of vision, and how to adapt these ideas for children with multiple disabilities.
1999, 76 pages, paperback, ISBN 0951752618
Available from University College London Institute of Child Health **www.gosh.nhs.uk**